NO AR

GIRLS' HEALTH ™

ONLINE SAFETY

JERI FREEDMAN

rosen publishing's
rosen
central®

Published in 2012 by The Rosen Publishing Group, Inc.
29 East 21st Street, New York, NY 10010

First Edition

Library of Congress Cataloging-in-Publication Data

Freedman, Jeri.
Online safety/Jeri Freedman.
    p. cm.—(Girls' health)
Includes bibliographical references and index.
ISBN 978-1-4488-4577-4 (library binding)
1. Internet and teenagers—Safety measures—Juvenile literature. 2. Online social networks—Juvenile literature. 3. Internet—Safety measures—Juvenile literature. 4. Cyberbullying—Juvenile literature. 5. Girls—Life skills guides—Juvenile literature. I. Title.
HQ799.2.I5F74 2012
004.67'808352—dc22

                                                                                    2011006531

Manufactured in the United States of America

CPSIA Compliance Information: Batch #S11YA: For further information, contact Rosen Publishing, New York, New York, at 1-800-237-9932.

CONTENTS

INTRODUCTION

The online world is no different from the physical world in terms of the precautions one should take. Just like the physical world, the online world contains its share of predators, criminals, and scam artists. Girls are particularly vulnerable because of their youth, attractiveness, emotional sensitivity, and perceived difficulty in defending themselves.

There are various types of individuals engaged in illegal activities on the Internet. Categories include: sexual predators (criminals that seek to seduce victims); hackers and identity thieves (criminals that steal users' personal information for financial gain); criminals that sell real and fake products; and criminals that seek to defraud users of their money outright.

It is not unusual for young women to be contacted via social media, texting, or e-mail by individuals seeking personal information or sexual interest. Such individuals use a variety of tricks to get the responses they desire. It is important to recognize the signs that an online contact may be a criminal or predator.

Not so long ago, people primarily accessed the Internet via desktop or notebook computers. Now, a variety of small handheld devices such as smartphones allow users to access the Internet, and each other, from anyplace, anytime. Similarly, the evolution from wired to wireless communications has made it easier for people to identify others' locations and access their information.

There are many things that girls must consider today when exchanging information over the Internet: how to keep their information safe from those not intended to know it, how to protect their privacy, and how to protect themselves and their money.

Today online predators and criminals can access victims on the Internet almost anywhere. Being prepared means knowing how to respond to inappropriate or shady contact.

This book explains the many security risks that girls encounter online when using a computer, smartphone, or other device. It also provides suggestions on how girls can protect themselves and their information and use the Internet safely.

CHAPTER one

THE RISKS OF ONLINE COMMUNICATION

According to a 2009 survey by Cox Communications and the Pew Internet & American Life Project, 93 percent of youth in the United States are online and 73 percent have a cell phone. Social networking sites such as Facebook, Twitter, and the like provide teenagers with a venue for sharing their lives and experiences. To a large extent, online communication through such sites has become the primary means of communication between young people. Despite the apparent friendliness on social media sites, dangers do lurk there.

There are major differences between online media and other forms of media used for communication. In a 2009 article in the *School Library Journal*, Ann Collier discussed the ideas of social media expert Danah Boyd. Boyd has identified some of the key characteristics of online media. They include:

- **Persistence**—The tendency of whatever is placed on the Internet to remain there permanently.

- **Searchability**—The ability of other people to locate information placed on the Web.

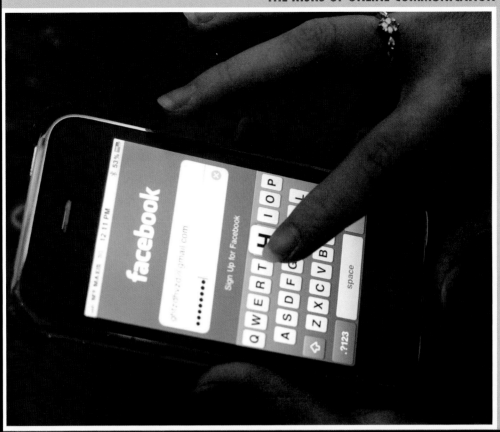

Content on social networking sites can go "viral," spreading anywhere and everywhere. When logging on, consider what would happen if the wrong person were to see your posts.

- **Replicability**—The fact that information placed on the Internet can be copied to other sites.

- **Scalability**—The fact that information on the Internet is reaching an ever-increasing audience.

All of these factors are issues that you should think about when communicating and sharing personal information over the Internet.

Citizens' groups around the country are working to pass legislation against sexting, cyberbullying, and other destructive online activities. Casi Lumbra, a volunteer with Teenangels, presents her group's research in Washington, D.C., in 2009.

ANYONE MAY BE YOUR FRIEND

In reality, far more people may be viewing the information posted on social networking sites than users realize. Some social networking sites suggest "friends" whom you can invite to join your site. These friends are often recommended on the flimsiest of pretexts—because they work or live in the same area as you, or have "friends" or other elements in common with you. If you are not careful whom you invite, you may give access to people that you do not actually know or trust. On the flip side, many young people who receive invitations to join other people's lists of "friends" accept all such invites. They assume that because they are invited, they actually know the person in question in some way. However, such friends may actually be strangers who are not well-disposed toward them.

REVEALING TOO MUCH

When it comes to risky online behavior, users are often their own worst enemies. Ill-thought-out communications and postings can have troublesome effects on their lives in the future.

One issue has to do with the way people—especially girls—choose to present themselves online. Everyone likes to feel attractive and be admired. However, one should carefully consider what is appropriate when it comes to posting photos and writing text. Sexting (the e-mailing or instant messaging of sexy photos and the posting of such photos online) is an area of concern for

Posting sexy pictures online can result in a barrage of inappropriate requests and attention, as well as harassment and bullying from peers.

several reasons. First, it can give a girl's peers the idea that she is willing to engage in sexual activity, which can make her a target for requests for sex. It can also make her the target of harassment or bullying by peers and the subject of rumors. Even worse, sexting can attract the interest of predators.

Posting sexy pictures of one's friends has even more pitfalls. Even if a friend gives permission to post the images, sharing the pictures can get the poster in trouble. Posting and e-mailing sexy photos of minors is a violation of child pornography laws, which are enforced very rigorously. Anyone—even a teen—found guilty of sending or posting such photos can end up with a criminal record as a sexual predator. Such a record lasts for years and affects the rest of a person's life. Further, there are serious penalties for sexting a picture of a peer to embarrass or bully her. School authorities are taking strong steps to stamp out bullying, and law enforcement may also become involved.

A ROADMAP FOR PREDATORS: TMI!

A second issue is providing too much information about one's life or property. Providing details about personal characteristics such as wealth can encourage criminals to target a girl or her family. Suppose you post photos of your home, with your address or the name of your town, and then you blog about leaving for a vacation. This tells potential thieves exactly when and where they might be able to break in and get away with it.

Some social networking sites have applications that let users broadcast where they are or will be at a certain time. Providing this information to the general public, combined with information about your money or attractive pictures of yourself, sends a complete package to online predators and crooks.

Digital photos taken with smartphones often contain embedded information about where they were taken. This feature can be disabled on cameras. However, if it isn't, posting a picture will reveal your location to anyone with an app that reads the global positioning system (GPS) information in the photo.

Most social networking and instant messaging (e-mail, chat, and texting) applications have an options or preferences menu. Within this menu, users often have the option to let certain people access their site, while blocking others. You should read the instructions for using these options in all applications. Use them to restrict access to only people you know and trust.

WOULD YOU WANT YOUR MOTHER TO HEAR THAT?

A good rule of thumb is not to write or post anything you wouldn't want your mother to see on television. Everything posted on the Internet is there forever. Information with your name on it is picked up by all types of indexing utilities for Web services ranging from Google to Wikipedia. In addition, people can link photos on friends' pages to their own profiles or even to Web sites outside the social networking site. Thus, you may find one of your photos showing up all over the Web—and it will still be there years later, when it is even more embarrassing. Once a photo or comment on a personal page has spread across the Internet, it is often impossible to get rid of it just by removing it from the original social networking page.

More and more employers are doing online searches for information about job applicants. Negative or embarrassing photos or text posted now may come back to haunt you in the future, keeping you from getting a position you want. Similarly, it is becoming more common for admissions reviewers at colleges and universities to check online for information about applicants.

CHAPTER two

CREEPS AND CRIMINALS: ONLINE PREDATORS

While young women can make many positive connections online, they need to be on the lookout for people who mean them harm. Predators are those who take advantage of others. Unfortunately, the Internet provides many opportunities for people who seek to take advantage of others physically, emotionally, or financially. By operating with awareness and caution online, girls can steer clear of predators.

SEXUAL PREDATORS

Sexual predators are individuals who prey on people for sexual purposes. Most sexual predators who hunt for victims over the Internet are not violent criminals seeking to abduct a girl. More often, they work by developing a rapport with their prey. They pretend to appreciate and sympathize with a girl in order to get her to send suggestive photos or agree to meet with them in person.

In a 2009 article by Anne Collier in the *School Library Journal*, David Finkelhor, director of the Crimes Against Children Research Center (CCRC) at the University of New Hampshire, explains, "These are not violent sex crimes. They are criminal seductions that take advantage of common teenage vulnerabilities. The offenders play on teens' desires for romance, adventure, sexual information, and understanding."

Also, according to CCRC's 2008 study, many sexual predators preying on young people are not adults but other young people seeking to lure the victim into a sexual relationship. According to CCRC researchers, "They take time to develop the trust and confidence of victims so that the youth see these relationships as romances or sexual adventures. The youth most vulnerable to online sex offenders have histories of sexual or physical abuse, family problems, and tendencies to take risks both online and offline." The study found that the activity that made young people most vulnerable was talking about sex online to people they did not know, through chat rooms, instant messaging, or e-mail.

Teens who feel lonely and isolated are particularly vulnerable to the attentions of online predators, who use sympathy and flattery to lure them into a relationship.

In most cases in which the predator is older than the target, the young people know they are talking to someone older than themselves. This, in itself, can be to the predator's advantage because a young person can be flattered by or desperate for the attention of an older person. Most predators seek to seduce young girls. However, the CCRC study found that nearly a quarter of the victims were young men, most of whom were gay or questioning their sexuality.

Online predators often fake an interest in books, movies, games, or other topics that the target is interested in. In many cases, they will eventually try to persuade the young person to send sexual material, such as photos. If the predator gets a victim to meet in person, this could put the victim at risk. Therefore, it is important to avoid giving personal information, such as an address, to people you chat with online but don't know personally. Don't give out your phone number to people that you meet online: it can be used to do a reverse lookup of your address. Also, don't grant strangers access as "friends" on your social networking pages, especially if your profile contains information that could help someone locate you, such as your address, school, or schedule.

SAFE CONTACT ONLINE AND OFF

Someday you may choose to meet with another teen that you met online through a social networking or gaming site. If you do, discuss this person with an adult. Check out anyone you meet online, or have your parents do so, through one of the online background-checking sites. Only agree to meet in a public place, and have a parent accompany you to the meeting. If a parent takes you there, he or she can make sure that the person you are meeting is safe. A person who does not mean you harm will understand that it makes sense not to meet a stranger alone. For the same reason, it makes sense to take friends with you to meet someone new. Not only is it safer to do things in a group, but your friends can also provide you with objective feedback about the person you are meeting.

When meeting with someone you get to know online, invite the person to do something with you and your friends in a public place. Make sure your parents know.

It's a good idea to check out anyone you don't know before engaging in any activity or sharing information with that person. Check with people you know in the community, and search Google for information about this person. Ask for access to his or her social networking pages, and see if the information there corresponds to other online sources, such as phone and address listings. Remember that it's not only adults masquerading as young people whom you need to be wary about meeting. Other young people or teenagers could be engaging in activities that are not safe.

Never meet someone you don't know by yourself, and never go anywhere without letting other people know where you are going. Always let your parents know, in person or by phone, text, or e-mail, where you are going and who is going with you. If you decide to go to a different location, call, text, or e-mail your parents to update them. If for any reason you can't reach your parents, let someone else (such as a friend's parents) know where you are going and with whom, and let them know that it is OK to share that information with your parents.

FINANCIAL PREDATORS

Not all online predators are after sex. Many are after users' money. While many reputable companies have online sites where they sell their products, there are also unscrupulous people selling products online. These fake

Law enforcement organizations monitor Web sites in order to identify those involved in illegal activity such as selling drugs, engaging in fraud, or committing crimes against children.

merchants may pretend to sell legal goods such as electronic devices. Or they may offer to sell goods that skirt the law, such as pirated software or steroids that enhance one's appearance. The sellers often contact potential customers through e-mail, ads on Web sites, or classified ad listings. They often offer popular products at exceptionally low prices.

Because the sellers are individuals, not recognized companies, there is no guarantee that you will receive the products you purchase. Further, a seller who offers to take a credit card payment may actually be seeking to obtain credit card numbers for the purpose of identity theft. For this reason, it's best to purchase products only from the sites of reputable companies. If you do make purchases from a small company's Web site, make sure the seller is verified by a third-party authority such as VeriSign. Always remember that if an offer seems too good to be true, it probably is.

Some teens and adults are tempted to buy illicit products online. They may wish to save money, as in the case of fake goods like pirated software. Or they may be lured by the promise of personal transformation in ads or e-mails for steroids or personal improvement products. Buying such products contributes to the growth of criminal activity and hurts the manufacturers of legitimate products. This can lead to negative consequences, such as the loss of jobs or increased prices for goods.

There are two other kinds of risk involved in purchasing illegal products. First, there are dangers to the individual doing the purchasing. For example, the seller may simply keep the purchaser's money and not send the goods, or the seller may send goods that do not work. In the case of pharmaceuticals or steroids, the product may be adulterated or completely fake, making it dangerous to use. A second risk is having a run-in with law enforcement. Police routinely monitor sites such as chat rooms to attempt to catch those involved in trafficking illegal products. Postal inspectors, working with law enforcement, check packages coming from known Internet suppliers of illegal products. People receiving the packages may find themselves in trouble as well.

MYTHS
AND
FACTS

MYTH   **Online predators are always older men.**

FACT   Many online predators are teens preying on other teens, so it's best to be cautious when dealing with any stranger online.

MYTH   **I have a right to get revenge by bullying a person online if he or she hurt me first.**

FACT   It is never acceptable to engage in bullying. If you think you have been treated unfairly, speak to your parents or teachers, and try to resolve the problem constructively.

MYTH   **If I have antivirus software on my computer, my computer is safe.**

FACT   Antivirus software alone does not protect against every threat. Software that provides a full package of security applications, including a firewall and anti-spyware utilities, is a better choice.

CHAPTER three

ONLINE BULLYING

According to StopCyberbullying.org, "Cyberbullying is when a child, preteen, or teen is tormented, threatened, harassed, humiliated, embarrassed, or otherwise targeted by another child, preteen, or teen using the Internet, interactive and digital technologies, or mobile phones."

Cyberbullying can take the form of a personal attack on an individual sent directly to that person. Alternately, it can take the form of embarrassing or hostile messages or photos distributed to others, such as schoolmates of the victim. Just as in physical bullying, cyberbullies can enlist their friends or classmates to participate in the cyberbullying.

A GROWING PROBLEM

The occurrence of online bullying has been increasing. According to a 2006 study by the National Center for Missing and Exploited Children, 9 percent of young people experienced online bullying in 2006, up from 6 percent five years earlier. According to the report, the number of youth who said they had "made rude or nasty comments to someone on the Internet" increased from 14 to 28 percent in the same period. The number who said they had "used the Internet to harass or embarrass someone they were mad at" increased from 1 to 9 percent.

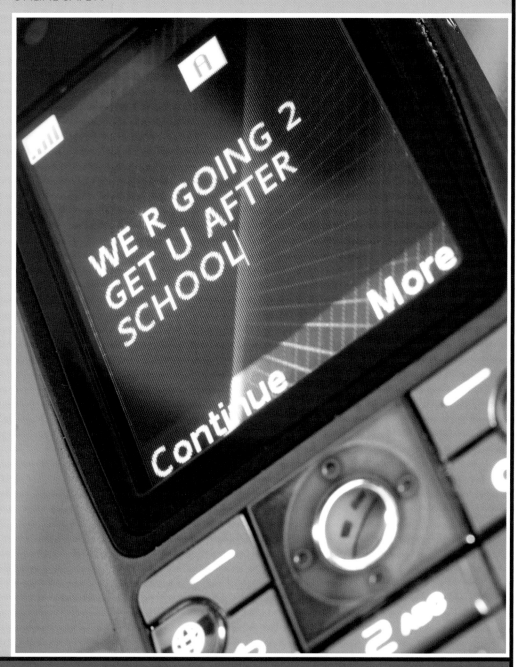

Cyberbullying is not harmless. It can lead to psychological problems, violence, and even suicide. It is impossible to take back harmful words once they have spread online.

Young people can engage in cyberbullying for any number of reasons, including revenge, anger, or resentment for some real or imagined slight. They might also become cyberbullies out of a sense of insecurity: they might hope to appear cool by picking on those who are deemed different or unattractive by their peers. For someone with low self-esteem, denigrating those with different traits can be a way to assert the superiority of one's own traits. Whatever its cause, cyberbullying has very negative effects.

THE EFFECTS OF ONLINE BULLYING

In one sense, the online world mirrors the real one: Nastiness leads to more nastiness, and kindness results in others being kinder. Treating people with respect and insisting that others do the same will make people respect you. Bullying others may give certain people a feeling of power. Although others may fear bullies, they won't like or respect them. In fact, even those who go along with bullying out of fear probably think that the bully is a creep. The fact is, people admire those who protect others more than those who hurt others. In addition, like other forms of abuse, online bullying often leads victims to strike out at others in the same way—by becoming aggressive. This creates an atmosphere that is disruptive and unpleasant for everyone. In extreme cases, cyberbullying has led to kids killing other kids or committing suicide.

One of the reasons why online bullying is so prevalent is the feeling of distance that communication over the Internet provides. One can say negative things about another person without having to look that person in the face and see the effect that one's words are having. Before you say anything cruel about another person online, ask yourself if you would say it in person. Ask yourself not only how the other person would feel, but also how you would feel if someone said it about you.

RESPONDING TO ONLINE BULLYING

The first thing to keep in mind is that a cyberbully is looking for a reaction. Therefore, one should not respond directly to the cyberbully. Instead, one of the first steps a victim can take is to block the sender's access. One can use the preferences or options features of social networking, e-mail, and texting applications to do this. Rather than engaging in an ever-escalating exchange of abuse with a cyberbully, warn the person that if the abuse does not stop, you will report it. If the bullying persists, do report it to the Internet service provider (ISP) or social networking site administrator.

Parents and school authorities have become very concerned about cyberbullying. Discuss online abuse with your parents so they can support you and take appropriate steps to stop it.

Cyberbullying is considered a serious problem, and if reported, bullies can lose their instant messaging, e-mail, or social networking account. They will then be blocked from accessing these services.

Discuss the situation with your parents. If they know the parents of the kids involved, they may be able to speak to them and have them stop the bullying. Also report the situation to school authorities, or have your parents do so. A school typically has no authority over bullying that occurs outside of school. However, online bullies often engage in in-person bullying as well, and school authorities can keep an eye out for such behavior. In addition, they can sometimes speak about the situation to the parents of the students involved, which may result in the parents taking action to stop the bullying. Most cyberbullying is aimed at embarrassing or humiliating the victim. However, if someone ever directly threatens you, tell your parents and school authorities immediately so that they can take appropriate steps.

Keep a sense of perspective. Although the situation is painful now, your school years will be a very small part of your entire life. Bullies often focus on superficial traits of their victims, such as height, weight, clothes, and athletic ability. In fact, those who do not fit in often turn out to be the most successful in adult life, when knowledge and skills are more important. As the poet George Herbert said, "Living well is the best revenge." Use your anger at bullying not to strike out at others, but to motivate you to excel at what interests you and do better than the bullies in the long run.

Flip through the pages of news and business magazines. The most successful people in the world are not those in *People* magazine. President Barack Obama is not only black and the child of a single mother, but his ears stick out, too. None of these things kept him from becoming president of the United States. A few seasons ago, Apple cofounder and multimillionaire Steve Wozniak appeared on the television show *Dancing with the Stars*. He said he did it because "I wanted to show that nerds can dance, too." This is a message to be taken to heart by anyone who is "different."

CHAPTER four

KEEPING YOUR DATA SAFE

One of the fastest-growing crimes today is identity theft, which is the act of stealing personal data to assume another person's identity. The most common motivation for doing this is to engage in illegal financial transactions. For example, an identity thief may use another person's identifying information to open fake credit card accounts and charge purchases to the victim. Identity thieves may also use personal information to produce false IDs, which they use to engage in criminal activity. Stolen Social Security numbers and other personal information can be used to target people for both illegal and legal, but annoying, activities. Therefore, it is important to protect your personal information.

PROTECTING YOUR DATA

The key to protecting your identity is protecting your personal data. There are a number of basic steps that you can take to keep your data from people who want to steal it. For example, don't store sensitive information such as credit card or Social Security numbers online, on your smartphone, or on your hard drive. Hackers—individuals who remotely enter people's computers for illegal purposes—have

Cyber criminals use a variety of software programs to search users' computers for passwords and other personal information they can use.

software that can search people's hard drives when they are online. They can also pick up information from wireless transmissions when people are using smartphones, such as iPhones, in public places.

Any computers you use should be protected by software that contains Internet security features. Such features include firewalls, which restrict access to your computer over the Internet, and antivirus software, which protects your computer from malicious programs. A number of companies, such as MacAfee and Symantec, make Internet security programs.

All smartphones have a password-protection feature. Using this feature can protect your data if your phone is lost or stolen.

USING A SMARTPHONE SAFELY

According to a Pew Research Institute study, 58 percent of twelve-year-olds have a cell phone and 83 percent of seventeen-year-olds have one. Today's smartphones, such as iPhones, BlackBerrys, and phones that run Google's Android software, allow users to text, send e-mail, and surf the Web. They also store a large amount of user information. They typically contain a record of names and addresses of people whom you know and a history of Web sites that you have visited recently. Many contain a note-pad feature, which many people use to record information that should be kept confidential. Smartphones present a unique danger because they are easily lost. If they fall into the wrong hands, they allow others to get hold of the data they contain.

One of the most basic ways to protect data on a smartphone is to use the password-protection feature that most phones provide. However, many people do not protect their phones in this way, because they don't want to bother unlocking their phone to use it. Furthermore, many people leave their phones on continuously so that they won't miss texts or phone calls. Thus, they are already logged in when a phone is lost.

Knowing all of this, there are additional steps that you can take to protect the data on your phone. Don't store passwords in the notepad or similar applications. In particular, don't store the passwords for your bank account or any sites, such as online gaming sites, to which you pay a monthly fee. People who find the phone could use banking pass-words to transfer money out of your bank account. Or they could set up accounts for themselves using your account information on pay-for-use sites. Use the same good password-setting rules you would use on a regular computer for accounts that you access through your smartphone, such as:

Set strong passwords to make it difficult for others to break into your accounts. Also change your passwords regularly, such as every three months.

- Don't use obvious usernames or passwords, such as your birthday or the name of a boyfriend. Likewise, don't use the name of a pet everyone around you knows about.
- Use a combination of capital and lowercase letters and at least one number.
- Use a variety of characters, including infrequently used letters such as "Q" and "X" and nonletter characters such as an exclamation point.

- Make the password as long as the site will allow. Using more characters makes it harder for a hacker to find the password through random trial.

Most smartphones have a feature that allows the user to back up page by page when searching the Internet. A person may log on to a site such as a banking Web site, gaming site, or online store, complete a transaction, and then go on to another Web site. In that case, it may be possible for someone else who gets hold of the phone to use the backup feature to return to the transaction site. Then the person could use the account to order things and have them sent to his or her address. Some sites, such as banks, automatically log users off after a certain period of time, but not all stores do this. Therefore, you should always log off of Web sites when you are finished using them.

However, logging off doesn't necessarily stop someone from backing up to a point before the log-off and viewing personal information. This data can include bank account balances or assets in investment accounts. When you have been visiting sites that contain sensitive information, you should always close the Web browser completely when you are done. This erases the browsing history and keeps others from seeing the pages you have used. The extra few seconds that one has to wait for the browser to open up again are worth the added security. If you do lose your phone, contact your service provider. The company may be able to access the phone remotely, regardless of where it is, and delete your data.

PROTECTING YOUR PRIVACY

Privacy policies are only good as long as they are in effect. It is not unusual for a new Web site—whether it be an online auction site, online merchant, gaming site, or social networking site—to promote itself at first as having a strong privacy policy for users' protection. However, such policies may not guarantee the privacy of your personal information in the long run.

One major threat to the privacy of your data is the possibility of security breaches. There have been numerous incidents in which hackers have breached Web sites' security and captured personal information, including credit card information. Individuals can do little to protect themselves from such professional security breaches, except respond to the news. If you hear that a security breach has compromised a Web site on which you have used a credit card (either your own or your parents'), have your parents contact the credit card company and get a new card number.

There is a second type of security issue that can arise. Sometimes the owners of Web sites change their security policies. Originally, a company's policy may have prevented the selling of your personal information to companies marketing products or services. Later, the company decides to change that policy. Information that a company may release to marketers includes your name, address, phone number, and demographic information, such as your age and gender. Sites may also report your personal interests, based on pages that you have visited or products that you have purchased. Pay close attention to notices from a company about such changes.

When legitimate online sites sell users' information to marketers, you generally have the option to opt out of participation. Many sites have an account preferences section in which you can request that your information not be shared with partners of the site. If the site that you are using has this feature, check the box to activate this option. However, be aware that if you use online sites, sooner or later whatever personal information you reveal on them may be shared with others.

10 GREAT QUESTIONS

1   Which software security programs should I install on my computer?

2   How do I get security updates for my computer?

3   What is a firewall, and how do I use one?

4   What settings should I use on my Web browser to provide the best security?

5   What spam-filtering programs are available to detect bogus e-mails?

6   How do I know if a Web site is safe for entering credit card information?

7   What security applications are available for my smartphone?

8   How do I turn off GPS encoding on my smartphone?

9   How can I be sure that my flash drive is free of viruses and other harmful programs?

10   How do I do an online background check on a person?

CHAPTER five

AVOIDING INTERNET SCAMS

Where there is money, there are criminals. The Internet is a vast storehouse of money in the form of stored credit card and bank account numbers, as well as personal data like Social Security numbers, that can be used to set up new accounts. Also, the Internet provides a rich venue for separating people from their money through fraud, or trickery.

SOCIAL ENGINEERING

To get users' bank account, credit card, or Social Security numbers, criminals often need individuals' usernames and passwords. Social engineering is one of the most common ways of getting a person's username and password. It involves manipulating someone through person-to-person contact with the intent of obtaining this information.

One common approach to social engineering involves the telephone. The crook calls the user, pretending to be a representative from his or her service provider. The criminal states that the company is implementing a feature upgrade or security enhancement that requires the person's username and password in order to be activated. Never give your username or password to anyone who

The Federal Bureau of Investigation (FBI) is actively engaged in tracking down identity theft rings. FBI officials in Los Angeles announce the arrest of dozens of people in 2009.

contacts you in this way. Instead, call the company directly—using their published number, not any number the scam artist gives you—and ask if it is doing such an upgrade. Then report the scam to the company's fraud department. It is virtually unheard of today for a legitimate company to ask for your username and password. It is also unlikely that it will ask you for your full Social Security number; in most cases, you will only be asked for the last four digits. Be suspicious of anyone who asks you for this type of information.

PHISHING

The same rules apply to requests for personal information via e-mail or instant messaging. The attempt to get usernames and passwords, account numbers, or Social Security numbers through these services is called "phishing." Scam artists have become adept at copying the letterheads and logos of real companies like eBay, Amazon, PayPal, banks, and other well-known institutions. They send e-mails or instant messages using the copied logos, along with statements designed to motivate the recipient to respond immediately. For instance, they might state that your account has experienced suspicious activity and will be closed if you don't log in and verify your identity. Alternatively, a message may tell you there was a problem with your payment for an item and that your order will be canceled if you don't log in and deal with the issue. Usually such messages include a link you are supposed to click to provide your information. If you click the link, you will be connected to the scammer's Web site, with a form designed to capture your personal information.

Never, ever click on the link in any e-mail that asks you to log in for any reason. If you think that there might be a real problem, go to the company's Web site the way you normally would, and then log in and check your account. Or call the company's online customer service number and ask them about the message. Again, a message from a legitimate company will not ask for your personal information. It will tell you to go to its site and log in to your account.

SPOOFING

Fake Web sites that mimic real sites, also called spoofed sites, provide scammers with another way to obtain people's usernames and passwords. Once the scammers have these, they can use them to access the victims' real accounts. Some fraudulent Web sites are set up to lure customers directly and then capture their personal data on a registration form. Such sites may be linked to ads in e-mails or instant messaging, or they may be featured in online classified ads.

A common approach to getting users to access a fraudulent Web site is called "cybersquatting" or "typo-squatting." Scammers using this approach set up a fraudulent site that will come up when a person makes a common error in the name of a popular, legitimate Web site. Microsoft gives the following examples of mistyped versions of its legitimate address: http://www.mircosoft.com and http://www.micosoft.com. When a user accidentally enters one of these mistyped versions, a fraudulent Web site may come up. If the user logs in to the site without carefully checking that the site is correct, the scammer captures the person's username and password. The scammer can then access the real site in the future, using that user's account.

Fraudulent sites frequently mimic financially lucrative sites, such as online auction sites, payment services such as PayPal, online merchants, and banks. Typing your username and password into one of these sites could give scammers access to money in your legitimate accounts. The scammers might also be able to charge things to the credit cards that you have registered at online merchants' sites. In addition, some spoofed sites contain fake offers, inviting you to sign up for new credit cards or bank accounts. Providing the necessary personal information will allow scammers to use that information in crimes of identity theft.

Before typing your username and password into any site, check that the site looks exactly the way it did the last time that you visited it. Many spoofed sites are not laid out exactly like the sites that they mimic. Also, check the spelling of the name of the site. Many fake sites used the mis-spelled versions of the legitimate site's name in their own logo, presumably for some sort of legal protection. Thus, if you type http://www.pypal.com instead of http://www.paypal.com, you will get a spoofed site, but the name on the site will actually be given as Pypal.com. So if you take the time to look, it will be obvious that you are on a spoofed site. If you have any doubts that a site is correct, retype the address and try again.

Many companies that provide security software for PCs, such as Symantec and MacAfee, provide complete Internet security products that include applications for identifying fraudulent Web sites. If you are searching the Internet today, it is much better to use a product that provides Internet security as well as antivirus protection, rather than antivirus protection alone. In addition, some Web browsers, such as Internet Explorer 8, include an application that helps identify spoofed Web sites.

Bank of America **Higher Standards**

Online Banking Alert

Need additional up to the minute account information? Sign In »

Change of Email Address

Your primary e-mail address for Bank of America Online Banking has been changed.

Did You Know? You can change your address, order checks and more online. Sign in to Online Banking and click on the "Customer Service" tab.

Because your reply will not be transmitted via secure e-mail, the e-mail address that generated this alert will not accept replies. If you would like to contact Bank of America with questions or comments, please **sign in to Online Banking** and visit the customer service section.

Bank of America, N.A. Member FDIC. Equal Housing Lender
© 2004 Bank of America Corporation. All rights reserved

Official Sponsor 2000-2004
U.S. Olympic Teams

To stop identity theft, many banks now inform you by e-mail when your account information is changed or when money is transferred.

PLOYS TO GET YOUR MONEY

E-mail and instant messaging provide a rich area for fraud. Some scams are straightforward attempts to get you to purchase something that will never be delivered. For instance, a seller may offer to sell you jewelry, electronics, games, DVDs, or other products at radically discounted prices. Chances are you will never see the product and you will lose your money. Never give a credit card number to anyone selling items through

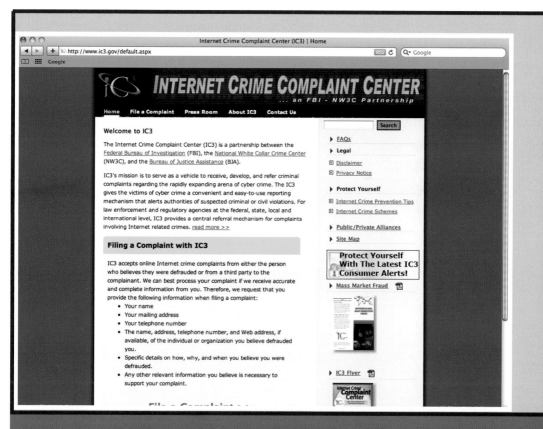

The Internet Crime Complaint Center (http://www.ic3.gov) allows people to file complaints of online fraud and identity theft. The site provides tips on how to avoid being a victim of Internet crime.

e-mail or instant messaging. Only use credit cards on sites that you know and trust—sites that have security procedures in place to protect your information.

Another common ploy that relies on e-mail and instant messaging is sending messages informing people that they have won a contest or lottery. These messages say that you must provide personal information to obtain your prize. Remember, you will never win a contest that you didn't enter. Never provide information in response to such a message. In a related scam, an individual sends a message claiming to have a large amount of money in an account. The message states that your help is needed to access the account in return for a share of the proceeds. Your help involves sending money. This is nothing but a scam to get your cash.

The Internet Crime Complaint Center (http://www.ic3.gov) is an online resource provided by the FBI, the National White Collar Crime Center, and the Bureau of Justice Assistance. Internet crimes can be reported on this Web site. Always remember: your safety depends on pro-tecting your personal information. So always practice safe surfing when using online resources.

adulterated Mixed with another substance, possibly harmful to the user.

aggressive Pushy, violent, or overly forceful.

antivirus software Software that protects a computer against viruses.

application A program for performing activities on a computer or online.

blog A running diarylike commentary online.

cyberbullying Online bullying.

cybersquatting Registering or using a domain name with intent to profit from someone else's trademark.

denigrate To belittle or put down someone else.

evolution Ongoing development.

firewall A software application that limits access to a person's computer over the Internet.

fraud The act of providing false information in order to trick people out of something valuable, such as money.

global positioning system (GPS) A system of orbiting satellites that uses wireless technology to track the location of receivers on Earth.

hacker A person who hacks, or gains access to, computers for illegal purposes.

identity theft The illegal use of others' personal identifying information, such as credit card or Social Security numbers, in order to get money or credit.

instant messaging Communicating via texting or online chat.

Internet service provider (ISP) The company that provides Internet service to a person's computer or smartphone.

legitimate Legal.

malicious Bad or evil.

phishing The act of tricking people into sharing information by sending fake e-mails or text messages.

pornography Material distributed for sexual purposes.

restrict To limit.

reverse lookup Using a physical or online directory to match an address to a phone number.

rigorously Strictly.

sexting Sending sexy photos or commentary via e-mail, text, or instant messaging.

smartphone A cell phone that also provides computerlike services such as texting, online chat, e-mail, and Internet access.

social engineering In computing, manipulating people through trickery to obtain information such as passwords.

social networking Communicating with others via electronic media to exchange information or socialize.

spoofing Sending a fake e-mail or setting up a fake Web site that looks as if it belongs to a real company.

utility A computer program that provides a particular function to a larger computer program or system, such as search "bots" that search the Internet for information and return it to a search engine.

virus A program planted on a computer to cause problems or steal information.

FOR MORE INFORMATION

Anti-Defamation League (ADL)
605 Third Avenue
New York, NY 10158
Web site: http://www.adl.org
This organization, which fights all kinds of bigotry, provides information on dealing with issues such as cyberbullying and hate
crimes. Its Web site provides a directory of local offices.

Council of Better Business Bureaus (BBB)
4200 Wilson Boulevard, Suite 800
Arlington, VA 22203-1838
(703) 276-0100
Web site: http://www.bbb.org
The Better Business Bureau provides resources for checking that a
business in the United States or Canada is legitimate.

Identity Theft Resource Center
9672 Via Excelencia, #101
San Diego, CA 92126
(858) 693-7935
Web site: http://www.idtheftcenter.org
This organization provides education on and assistance with identity
theft. Its Web site includes a Teen Space.

Information and Privacy Commissioner, Ontario
2 Bloor Street East, Suite 1400
Toronto, ON M4W 1A8
Canada

(800) 387-0073

Web site: http://www.ipc.on.ca

The Information and Privacy Commissioner educates the public about Ontario's access and privacy laws.

National Center for Missing & Exploited Children (NCMEC)

Charles B. Wang International Children's Building

699 Prince Street

Alexandria, VA 22314-3175

(703) 224-2150

Web site: http://www.missingkids.com

The NCMEC serves as a resource on the issues of missing and sexually exploited children. The organization provides information and resources to law enforcement, parents, children, and other professionals.

National Crime Prevention Council (NCPC)

2001 Jefferson Davis Highway, Suite 901

Arlington, VA 22202

(202) 466-6272

Web site: http://www.ncpc.org

The NCPC organization provides information and resources for students and parents in dealing with cyberbullying, identity theft, and other crimes.

National Organizations for Youth Safety (NOYS)

7371 Atlas Walk Way, #109

Gainesville, VA 20155

(828) 367-6697

Web site: http://www.noys.org

NOYS provides information on youth safety, including bullying prevention and Internet safety, and sponsors a variety of events and youth leadership projects.

WEB SITES

Due to the changing nature of Internet links, Rosen Publishing has developed an online list of Web sites related to the subject of this book. This site is updated regularly. Please use this link to access the list:

http://www.rosenlinks.com/gh/safe

FOR FURTHER READING

Allman, Toney. *Mean Behind the Screen: What You Need to Know About Cyberbullying*. Minneapolis, MN: Compass Point Books, 2009.

Arata, Michael J. *Identity Theft for Dummies*. Hoboken, NJ: Wiley, 2010.

Bailey, Diane. *Cyber Ethics* (Cyber Citizenship and Cyber Safety). New York, NY: Rosen Publishing, 2008.

Cindrich, Sharon. *A Smart Girl's Guide to the Internet: How to Connect with Friends, Find What You Need, and Stay Safe Online* (Be Your Best). Middleton, WI: American Girl, 2009.

Criswell, Patti Kelley. *Stand Up for Yourself and Your Friends: Dealing with Bullies and Bossiness and Finding a Better Way*. Middleton, WI: American Girl, 2009.

Gardner, Olivia, Emily Buder, and Sarah Buder. *Letters to a Bullied Girl: Messages of Healing and Hope*. New York, NY: Harper, 2008.

Humphrey, Sandra McLeod. *Hot Issues, Cool Choices! Facing Bullies, Peer Pressure, Popularity, and Put-Downs*. Amherst, NY: Prometheus Books, 2007.

Jacobs, Thomas A. *Teen Cyberbullying Investigated: Where Do Your Rights End and Consequences Begin?* Minneapolis, MN: Free Spirit Publishing, 2010.

Levete, Sarah. *Taking Action Against Internet Crime* (Taking Action). New York, NY: Rosen Publishing, 2010.

Ludwig, Trudy. *Confessions of a Former Bully*. Berkeley, CA: Tricycle Press, 2010.

MacEachern, Robyn. *Cyberbullying: Deal with It and Ctrl Alt Delete It*. Toronto, Canada: J. Lorimer & Company, 2008.

McGraw, Jay. *Jay McGraw's Life Strategies for Dealing with Bullies.* New York, NY: Aladdin, 2008.

Orr, Tamra. *Privacy and Hacking* (Cyber Citizenship and Cyber Safety). New York, NY: Rosen Publishing, 2008.

Sandler, Corey. *Living with the Internet and Online Dangers* (Teen's Guides). New York, NY: Facts On File, 2010.

Singer, Alexis. *Alexis: My True Story of Being Seduced by an Online Predator.* Deerfield Beach, FL: Health Communications, 2010.

Sommers, Michael A. *The Dangers of Online Predators* (Cyber Citizenship and Cyber Safety). New York, NY: Rosen Publishing, 2008.

INDEX

ABOUT THE AUTHOR

Jeri Freedman has a B.A. from Harvard University. For fifteen years, she worked for high-technology companies. She is the author of more than thirty young adult nonfiction books, many published by Rosen Publishing. Among her previous titles are *Privacy vs. Security*, *Cyber Citizenship: Intellectual Property*, and *Women in the Workplace: Wages, Respect, and Equal Rights*.

PHOTO CREDITS